Contents

DEDICATION:

∞∞∞

I would like to dedicate this book to my mother Frencilla Holden. She has always been there for me in my time of need. She is one of the most strongest woman I know. Part of who I am today is because of her. She is a loving mother, wife, and grand-mother. In this book you will recieve only partial of her motherly love. Thank you mother for loving me and teaching me how to be strong and go for what I want in life. I love you so very much. You are my everything.

I would also like to dedicate this book to Mrs. Woodward. You've helped me remember who God is and what he is capable of doing for us through faith. I really appreciate you so much. Thank you for everything you have ever done for me and my daughter. Even fifteen years later you are still encouraging me. Thank you!

Last, but not least I would also like to dedicate this book to my amazing daughter D'ziyah. You have made me the woman I am today. I love you so very much my sweetness. You really keep me together and encourage me by your strength. Never stop reaching for the stars baby girl, because you can complete any dreams or goals you want. I believe in you always and support you. I am so thankful to be your mother.

Welcome to New York!

∞∞∞

O*h Yes!* I remember this like it was yesterday! It was me, my mom and three of my sisters. We just moved from South Carolina to New York City. Many problems occurred which left my mother no choice, but to take us to a shelter. We went to three different locations, until we actually had a good placement in Jamaica, Queens. My mom signed us all up for a school called P.S. 217, except my oldest sister. She went to high school a little further up the street.

Yes! Eighth grade I couldn't wait to start. The first couple of weeks went by so smooth. Then one day while in school these two popular girls in my class room got upset with me, because I was answering so many questions. They started whispering about me, but I could hear them. So, when they said they were going to "press me" (which means angrily speak to me) when we exit the building I went into a rage. I picked up a chair and threw it at them while charging their way. As soon as I got in contact with them I begin punching them and screaming, "Press me now! Press me now!". The rage I felt, I thought came from just moving from the only place I knew in the world, missing all my friends, or maybe just from living in a shelter. I just couldn't stop fighting them. I was so angry, until the point where I injured two teachers and a security guard while they were trying to break the fight up. They finally got me off the girls and took me to the Principal's office. The principal was angry and called my mother immediately! At that point I did not even care and I kept telling the principal that too. Then another security guard pulled me out the office, because I was crying so much that I couldn't speak. When he pulled me out the office he begged me to calm down, but I couldn't. At that moment I asked myself why can't I calm down!

Thoughts started running thru my head of me being pregnant, but it did not stay there for long! The security guard ended up calming me down and I immediately thought about my mother coming to the school angry as hell. As soon as I thought that, then guess who walked in the school. She looked so angry!! We were called into the principal's office where they told my mother that I was being suspended for ninety days. Shaking my head! I thought my mother was going to kill me. She signed the suspension papers and we went home. Everyday after that my sisters went to school without me.

The Disappointment

∞∞∞

Like two weeks went by and I noticed I didn't get my period for a couple of months. I was so afraid and did not know what to do. I thought about it day and night from sun up to sun down. I finally came to the conclusion that I had to tell my mom, because my belly was getting a little pudge. One day after my sisters left for school I started cleaning the entire house just like my mother liked it. Then, I sat on my bed and wrote her a letter telling her what was going on and how I felt inside. I waited till she went to the store and got breakfast to make for us, and placed the letter on her bed. I went into my room and waited. She returned from the store and called my name out to help her with the bags. I put the grocery away so fast, because I felt like I couldn't see her face of disappointment when she read the letter. I went back into my room and prepared for her to bust into my room throwing hits at me. Then, I heard her crying softly in her room. It felt like she cried for hours, but it was about ten to twenty minutes until she calmed down and called me into her room. I felt my heart drop, because I knew she probably was just as disgusted and disappointed in me as I was in myself. She sat me down and started to cry then I cried. We talked and cry some more, until she came up with a plan. She said we were going to the doctor, and we were going to figure this situation out together. Abortion was out the picture for her, but I didn't think she could actually afford another baby coming into our situation, so I did think about it. That same day she set a doctor's appointment for me for the following week.

The Doubt

∞∞∞

The following week arrived and she got all my sisters ready for school and out the door they went. Then we began to get ready to go to the doctor and mommy didn't seem so mad anymore. She told me that no matter what happens that she loved me, and we were going to get through this together. So we went on our journey to the doctor's office. To get to the doctor's office we had to take two buses to South Jamaica, Queens which took forty-five minutes a piece. When we got off the first bus I was so hungry and mommy asked if I wanted something to eat. I asked to go to the McDonalds in front of the bus stop that we was waiting on. When we got inside mommy told me to get what I wanted, so I ordered the Big & Tasty meal. We sat down and ate there. She talked and I listened. I was so happy to have my mother there for me and I did not feel alone anymore. The first bite that I took felt like I was in Heaven. After we finished up our food we noticed the bus was coming and ran to the bus stop and got on the bus. We arrived to the doctor's office, and I was no longer afraid, just nervous. The doctor said that I was indeed three months pregnant. She offered the abortion and my mom spoke for me saying I did not want it. The doctor then explained the policy for a situation like mines. I was considered an adult in New York and I could make my own decisions when it came to my baby. Of course my mom was not trying to hear that. She argued with the lady. So bad that I was afraid of telling her that I may actually consider the abortion, so she wouldn't have to be superwoman because of me. Well we ended up leaving after they set up my prenatal care.

I felt so bad after that because everything started really hitting me. I was only thirteen going on fourteen years old, I did not have a job, and I needed to finish school. My mom would have to carry this burden on top of the situation she was going through. I couldn't believe that this was all because of me. My poor mom she was so strong for me.

My mom is the best. She would not let anyone hurt me. She made sure we ate even if that meant her not eating. Me and my sisters used to lie and say we were not hungry just so she could eat something. She was so strong. Always showing us that things were possible.

I want my Big & Tasty

∞∞∞

Being pregnant really changed me and my mother. It was like she was my baby father and mother. When there were left overs she would not let any of my sisters have it unless I said I didn't want it. They would really get in trouble because of it too. Looking at her and watching her struggle to stay strong and battle the world to protect all of us made me love her even more. She looked like an angel in my eyes and I always prayed for her.

She continued to take me to the doctor's office and buying me Big & Tasty meals. We bonded so much on those long bus rides and at my doctor's appointments. My appointments were every two weeks at the same time. One day in the morning before going to the doctor's office I heard mommy yelling at someone over the phone about money. She was very upset and I heard her say she was broke that day. So I just knew I was not getting my Big & Tasty. While we were leaving she said don't worry baby I will get you your McDonalds it just might be a little later. I told her I was okay and didn't really need it because I should be eating healthy anyways. I knew dam well I really wanted my Big & Tasty!

When we got off the first bus, and immediately stood by the second bus stop all I could do is try to not look at McDonalds. It was another hard thing I had to do. I could smell everything. My stomach was growling so much knowing what it wanted and not receiving it. I probably stopped myself like twenty times from crying to stay strong so I wouldn't make my mother upset. I just wanted to get on the bus, but the bus took like forty minutes to come. That hurt so much. Could you imagine being pregnant, hungry, broke, and trying to be strong. It was so horrible. We got on the bus and continued our journey to see the doctor.

Everything went great, except when the doctor said I was losing too much weight and I needed to eat more and take my prenatal pills. My mother said she didn't understand, but I knew exactly what it was. Every chance I got to get away from my mother I cried of guilt. I would cry for hours until I threw up from knowing that I put so much more stress on her, but I did not say anything about it. We went to the pharmacy and got my medicine after that. Then, mommy got a phone call and she said we were going to Money Gram, so we could go to get my McDonalds. I was so happy that I could taste the pickles from the sandwich. I got my McDonalds and fell in love with my mother all over again.

Time to Pray!

∞∞∞

Later that day when I was alone I broke down inside of the bathroom crying again thinking about everything. I remembered that my grandmother always told me that praying help fix things, so I dropped to my knees looking up to the ceiling crying. I started asking God that if it was meant for me to keep my child, then how would I take care of it. I told him about school and how all I did was feel pain everywhere I went. I told him about my mother's struggle and how I did not want to make it worst, then I asked him for help! I kept asking for reassurance over and over. Then I started to feel a little better and told myself that everything had to be okay.

My ninety days approached rapidly and it was time for me to go back to school. My belly was growing right along with the time. I was about six months pregnant, but considered to be small for those months. So when I started back at school I wore a big t-shirt so no one would know I was pregnant. The first day my mom had to come with me to the school to talk to the principal for my return. While speaking with the principal my mother told her about my pregnancy and she tried to explain to my mom that I would be uncomfortable there. She said it would also send the wrong message to the teens that attended the school. She started talking about an alternative school and I started getting very emotional again, because my mother was upset. My mother asked me if I wanted to go to an alternative school and I said no. She told the principal that I was staying at that school unless there are rules stating no pregnant teens could be there. I didn't think she wanted that kind of trouble with my mother so she allowed me to start the following day.

Back to school

∞∞∞

The next day I went back to school and I was so happy. I no longer wanted to stay home because I felt so depressed in there sometimes. When I arrive to school and went into P.E. class (also known as physical education class), the coach called me to the front. He said the guidance counselor needed to speak with me. The guidance counselor explained to me that I was far along in my pregnancy and it wouldn't be safe for me to attend the P.E. class anymore. She said they had a better idea and took me to a health class. I entered the class quietly, because I did not want anymore trouble for myself.

The health teacher name was Mrs. Woodward. The guidance counselor told me to sit down at an empty desk. Mrs. Woodward asked me to introduce myself to the class. I stood sitting down and told everyone my name. She thanked me for joining them and continued with her lesson. She pointed to a red box and said the box was called, "The suggestion box". She said if we had any questions or concerns then we could write it on a paper and place it in that box without writing our names on it. She said she would speak about the letters the following day. She then said the lesson for that day was about sex. A student started reading an article on sex that was given to all of us from Mrs. Woodward. While that student read someone said aloud, "How is a baby born", and everyone laughed. Mrs. Woodward said we will get to that later in the course and then started to joke with us saying we should not be worrying about having babies at the age we were. Then some students started saying that they didn't want children because of their futures. Others started saying that at 13 and 14 years old no one should be having sex because it was disgusting. I thought that coming to school would make me feel better, but that day I felt even more depressed. It took everything inside me to not break down at that very moment in front of the whole class. Then I remembered about the Suggestion Box and begin to write. I wrote, "Dear Mrs. Woodward, How do you know if someone is pregnant inside your class and you offended them today." Then the bell rang and class was over. I met up with my sisters after the next class and we went home on the yellow bus.

Thank God for her

∞∞∞

The next day I went to school and everything was fine until I went to lunch. I remembered just sitting down at a corner table alone preparing to eat my lunch when I noticed three security guards approaching me. They called my name and asked me to follow them. I remembered the letter I wrote for Mrs. Woodward, and was so afraid that I would get into trouble again. So, I asked the security guards what did I do. They said they didn't know, but I still had to come with them. I realize we were walking upstairs so I wasn't going to the principal's office. Then I notice the way they were escorting me was the way to Mrs. Woodward's class. To my surprise it was that classroom they were taking me.

When they told me to enter Mrs. Woodward was standing at a round table with Popeyes, Subway, and a McDonald's bags on the table. There was also a stack of papers there too. She then asked me to come inside and have a seat. As I walked to sit down she stared at my belly and started to cry. She apologized like a million times for the day before and gave me a big hug. I started crying with her thinking about how I felt that day and how the hug she gave me was the best apology in the world at that time. Her hug was so sincere just like my mother. So I sat at the table with her and she slid the Popeyes, Subways, and McDonalds to me and said these are for you. At that very moment I fell in love with her. How did she know I loved McDonalds!!

While I was eating she explained to me that she was a Christian. She said she could not have any children of her own, so she became a foster mom. She showed me photos of her foster children. I explained my situation to her as well and she told me everything was going to fine. I felt some kind of relief hearing that from her.

We both finished our meals, then that's when she told me she had something for me. She slid the stack of papers to me. She told me that the papers were coupons to get my nails and toes done for the remainder of my pregnancy. I started to cry thanking her. Then she asked me to write down what I needed for the baby and whether or not I was having a girl or boy. I told her we were unsure, but we would know in the next two to three weeks. She said, "Well then I guess we have to get unisex things." So on the paper she had given me I wrote down bottles and pampers. When I told her I was done she walked over and looked at the paper to see what I wrote. She looked up at me and said, "That's it! Do you have everything else?" I told her we didn't have anything yet until we learned the sex of the baby, but in all actuality we didn't even have much money. Then she sat next to me and said that we were going to write out a list and she would get what she could. That was fine with me, so we wrote out a four page list. She asked me if it was okay if she told her church my story and see if they would help and I was totally okay with that. Then class was about to start so I packed everything up and thanked her for everything. She told me I could always talk to her if I needed it. She also told me that everything was going to be okay and to trust that God could get me through anything. Class ended and I went home so happy and relieved. I don't remember telling my mom that night, but I do remember thanking God for sending me Mrs. Woodward.

A Blessing in Disguise

∞∞∞

The next day at lunch the same thing happened. Mrs. Woodward sent for me to come to her class. When I entered the class she grabbed me so tight and said God is everything!!! She grabbed my face and told me that when she told the church my story everyone gave so much money, and offered to help with the shopping too. She then told me she had bad news also. She said on the list they forgot specific bottles that we wrote down and started laughing. I was so happy and thankful and couldn't stop crying and looking up at God. She told me they all got together and went shopping and needed a large truck for the amount of stuff they had. I was so amazed and speechless at the same time. Then she told me to always keep my faith and never let anyone tell me otherwise. I couldn't wait to get home to tell my mother.

When I got home I told my mother about Mrs. Woodward, and what we talked about. She was so happy! I also told her I gave Mrs. Woodward her number to contact her. It was now the week-end and we were in the house playing with each other when my mom received a phone call asking for me and her to come outside. When we got in front of our building we saw a very large truck!! Two men and a women was standing in front it. I just knew the truck was from Mrs. Woodward. My mother looked at me with the biggest smile I have seen from her since we got to New York. As we walked to the people standing in front of the truck they all put their hands out to shake our hands and introduced their selves as Mrs. Woodward's church family. They said it was so nice to meet us and they had something very special for us!! They lift up the back of the truck and to our surprise it looked like Babies R Us in there. My mom covered her face in disbelief and I just started crying again looking at the sky saying to myself God why would you do this for me! Then they all hugged us and told us God is good all the time!! They would not let us carry anything into the house. The two men delivered everything inside. I couldn't believe the things I saw! Everything was brand new! Not one thing was used. They told us that they had more things to deliver the next day as well.

When they left, me and my mother went inside and we looked through all the stuff my mom dropped to her knees and started crying. I started smiling so much in disbelief of what God had done for us. I remembered leaving mommy for a second to go inside the bathroom, and I did the same thing she did. I dropped to my knees and cried to God thanking him a bunch of times. I felt so alive and full of relief. I finally felt like I could really do the mommy thing. I returned back to the kitchen where my mother was and we started opening stuff and setting the baby things up. It was late, but we did not care. We were so happy and too busy bonding that we didn't even notice the time. Opening the boxes and seeing the stuff they brought for the baby we were confused on what else they needed to bring, because everything was more than we had imagined.

The next day when I went to school Mrs. Woodward was absent so I didn't get see her. When I arrived home two hours later my mom received another phone call telling us to come outside again. To our surprise it was another large truck full of stuff. I couldn't believe it. I was too over whelmed by the feelings I had inside. It was like the baby knew what was happening and the baby was so blessed. They delivered the rest of the things into the house and left ,telling us they had one more delivery for the next day. After we went through all the stuff we realized that the baby had two of everything. The shelter people even said they have never seen anything like it before. That night I slept like a baby with my baby, and I excepted the fact that that's exactly what I was in my mom's eyes.

I love you more

∞∞∞

The next day I saw Mrs. Woodward and I cried again. I ran into her arms with my big belly and screamed out loud, "Thank you so much". My knees got weak like I was about to faint. We sat down and ate some McDonalds' she brought, but this time she didn't bring the Popeyes. When I noticed I asked her why she brought more McDonalds', and no Popeyes this time, not to sound greedy. She laughed at me and said it's okay you can be greedy with me. Then she said the first time she noticed that I only ate the Big & Tasty meal and I looked like I really loved it so much. So this time she brought me two sandwiches. I fell in love with her all over again. I knew the only way of her knowing that without me telling her was God. I took a bite of one of my sandwiches and started crying. She asked what's wrong and I said I love Big & Tasty so much, but I love you even more. Thank you for everything.

We finished our food and it was time for class, so I cleaned my mess and stood by the door as if I just came in so other students wouldn't know what was going on. I let other students come in first and I stood second to last. When everyone sat done she asked for me to come to the front of the class. I was so afraid, but when I looked her in her eyes I knew it was okay. So I stood up and walked to her. When I got to the front Mrs. Woodward wrapped one hand around my shoulder and one around my belly, then said I would like to properly introduce a new student. She said, " This is Shanique Garland everyone. She is pregnant and she is strong. The other day we spoke about this in a horrible way and she heard it and it hurt her very bad. I would like all of us to apologize and continue these class lessons not being judgmentally towards nothing and no one. It was like the whole time she spoke the students was staring at my stomach with their mouths opened. Then their faces turned into sincerity. After Mrs. Woodward stop talking all the students got close to me apologizing to me, giving me hugs, and talking to me. It was amazing and I got so many new friends all in one day.

Lots of Friends

∞∞∞

When I arrived home, there was our last delivery! I couldn't imagine what else they could have brought. When they opened the back it was five very large boxes. They delivered them into the house and gave us both huge hugs. They told us that it was an honor meeting us. Me and mommy thanked them for everything, and we went into the house and hurried to see what was in the boxes. It was two beautiful bassinets, two strollers, and a crib!! Wow!! Wow! Wow!! Me and my mother stayed up again most of the night putting everything up talking and laughing. I finally was completely happy. Everything at school was going great, I got alot of new friends, my mother was happy, and my baby had everything I could ever imagine when she came into the world. Everything that I asked God for.

Everything was going great for me after that! My new friends loved me and protected me from everything and everyone. No one could tease me or say anything bad about me or my baby. When I went to different classes they would meet up with me and walk down the aisle surrounding me so no one could get close to my belly to bump it. One day we were eating lunch at the round table in the lunch room that I once sat alone at, and out of nowhere the two girls I fought walked over to the table. So my friends stood up and put their hands on my shoulder as if I shouldn't stand. The girls had a different look on their faces this time though. They looked sincere this time around, but I think I was the only one to noticed it. My friends looked like they wanted to attack them, but I said wait a minute guys and stood up. Well I tried to stand up on my own, but my friends helped me up. Then I walked to the girls and ask how could I help them.

They apologized to me and said they no longer wanted any problems. They also said they were wrong for picking on me and had no idea of my situation. They said they were suspended too and the whole thing taught them a serious lesson. They said they hope we could move forward and all be one team. Then they took their hands from behind their backs and both handed me gifts they brought for my baby. Of course I started crying cause that's all I did, then just ran to them and hug them. I apologized too just because it felt like the right thing to do, and inside I was wrong for throwing the chair and fighting them. At that time I just wanted love to surround me, so I had a burst of love to give.

Guidance

∞∞∞

After that I had a large crew, I was very popular, and my crew had to use manners around me, because being from New York they had none. The teachers started to notice the students behaving well and participating in class since they were hanging with me. The principal said the fights decreased. She pulled me in her office and thank me for coming to her school. She touched my belly and said you will be a great mom and you will go really far, just keep your manners and stay in school. I promised her I would and went to my next class. At the end of each day I always went to see Mrs. Woodward if I didn't have her class.

My belly was growing and growing. I stayed in school and everything was going great, until one day in Mrs. Woodward's class I started feeling weak and dizzy. It was like she knew because she stopped in the middle of the lesson and asked if I was okay. I reached for my head and she rushed over to me. The other students ran too. Some of them tried to help me up, but I felt a sharp pain in my back and stomach, so I couldn't stand. They called the nurse and my mother. The nurse joined us in the classroom and checked my vitals. The students found me water and milk. I drank everything, but I was still cramping. My mother arrived and asked if I was okay. She asked me if I needed to go to the hospital and I said yes because I wanted the baby to be safe, and I did not know what was going on. The ambulance arrived and we went to the hospital.

When we got there the nurses checked me and then the doctors checked me to see if I had dilated, but I didn't. They gave me 2 IVs and said I was very dehydrated. I didn't understand because of all the water I'd drunk thoughout my pregnancy. After I got hydrated it was time to go home. When me and my mom arrived home we wanted to go through the baby things again. So we did, then went to sleep.

The next day when I arrived at school my friends was so happy to see me and I felt the same way. A hour into the class the teacher asked me to go to the principal's office. When I arrived the principal asked me to have a seat and on the look of her face I knew it was bad. She told me that she think it was time for me to stay home until after the baby was born. Now, this was about early March so I knew I would never return to school, because New York schools end in June. I was in eighth grade, so I would never return at all after that year.

I was so emotional, but I knew she was right because the school told my mom that eighth graders could no longer ride the school bus anymore. So I had to walk to school. One day while walking ten blocks alone to the school in the snow I was so tired, so I cut through a basketball court. When I got to the stairs I walked down them softly holding the ramp because they looked slippery. After I got down those stairs there was a hill, so I started to walk down it, but not as softly as the stairs before and I fell down. I did not just fall down though I rolled like four times. When I stopped rolling I tried to see if I saw someone to help me up like my friends usually would do, but there was no one. I did not have a phone at the time to call my mother, so that was out of the picture. I was alone and I was hurt.

I tried my hardest to protect my stomach by holding it as I rolled, but on the last roll my arms broke loose. I lift my coat and shirt up to look at my belly and one side was good, but the other side was bruised. I pushed on my stomach to see if my baby would move like usual and I got kicked so hard. That kick hurt so much, but it made me the happiest girl in the world knowing my baby was okay. So I knew it was time for me to stop school. That was the reason I did not put up any fight with the principal when she told me. I just asked her since it was Thursday could I come to school the next day to say goodbye to everyone and she agreed. She said it was a honor meeting me and I was very special to all of them. She gave me a huge hug and told me to come see her the next day before I left so she could give me a gift for the baby.

Thank you God

∞∞∞

As I started walking down the hall back to the class I held one of my arms out and dragged it on the wall. It was like everything seemed so right for me. The colors of the walls were brighter than I remembered, the drawings from my peers were more beautiful and connected. It was like every painting, picture, and words on those walls were for me and me only. Then I began to smile . I got that tingly feeling in my belly like I wanted to cry, but I couldn't because something was not letting me. I knew exactly what it was so I just looked up and smiled and said thank you to God.

Then the bell rung and I was so excited because it was time for Mrs. Woodward's class. When I got to her door another lady was there. So I sat down while she introduced herself. She said she was a substitute and Mrs. Woodward would not be back until Monday! I was sad because she wouldn't get to see me before I left the next day. I was happy that my friends were there so I could tell them that I was leaving though. They were so sad when I told them but they said they would write me and call me. We all exchanged numbers and continue with the class.

I went home and told my mother, and she asked me if I was okay. I looked her in her eyes and said yes, so she knew I was really okay. I told her I wouldn't be able to see Mrs. Woodward before I left, and she said it was okay I could call the school to talk to her. She also said that we could visit the school after I had the baby, so that made me feel much better. The next day when I went to school we had one last lunch and it tasted like the best lunch we had since I been there. My friends was crying and we was choosing names for the baby. Then at dismissal they all walked me home. I felt so loved.

Our Secret

$\infty\infty\infty$

At this point there was no more school for me, so I had to stay home with mommy again. We went to the doctor every week instead of every two weeks because I was close to birth. When we got to the doctor we found out that we were having a girl. I was so happy. Then we went home after I got my Big and Tasty. It was great this time around, because we were getting ready for our princess's arrival. Me and mommy folded her little clothes seemed like everyday. Mommy did not want to put her bassinets up because they were white and she did not want no dirt on them. She let me call Mrs. Woodward at the school a lot of times and that made me very happy to know we were always in contact. I told her the sex of the baby and she was happy too. She couldn't wait until I had her because she wanted to see and hold her.

That day came and it was delivery time. The baby was due April 29, 2004, but she didn't come till May 4, 2004. I remember it so much because something very special happened that night. Prior to us coming to New York my oldest sister had a miscarriage. It was very depressing that her baby heart just stopped one day and we did not know why. She did nothing crazy. She didn't smoke or drink, so we was completely blinded by it. During my pregnancy she was very attached to me and wouldn't let anything happen to me either. Sometimes when I would cry in the stairwell in the shelter, she would always find me and sit with me and cry and made me laugh. Then she would say my butt is hurting from sitting on these concrete stairs Nene (that's what my whole family called me). We would laugh and she would help me up and we would go back into the house like nothing happened. That was always our little secret and I love her for keeping that secret for me till this day.

The morning I went into the hospital started off like every regular night at 4 am when I would go to the bathroom. This time on my way to the bathroom my legs got weak, I got dizzy, and I had those same sharp pains like before. I fell on the floor, but only made a little noise. My oldest sister peeked out the room to where I was and closed the door back instead of helping me up. I was in so much pain, but I knew something was wrong with her. So I gained the strength to get up and check on her. When I went into the room she was sitting on their bottom bunk of their bunk bed crying in the dark. So I closed the door halfway so I could use the light from the kitchen to see her. I sat next to her and asked her what was wrong. She said, "Why you get to keep your baby, but mines died. I was always the good one and you were always so bad. You even fought someone and your baby is still here. Why did my baby have to die?"

Now you know I got so emotional and started crying with her. I gave her a hug so tight not caring how much pain I was in because I once felt like I didn't want my baby and I knew she wanted hers. I told her that if I could give her my baby out my stomach I would, because she deserved her more than me. I told her I didn't know why God saved my baby and did not save hers, but she could have my baby if she wanted to if that would make her happy. She looked at me seeing all my tears, pain, and probably seeing that I was serious too, then she looked at my belly and said no. She said we could share her! We both laughed and wiped our tears and she said, "Come on girl let's go wake mommy up because you look like you are in so much pain." We laughed again and she helped me up. We woke mommy up and she called the ambulance and we went to the hospital.

Where is my baby?

∞∞∞

It seemed like it took forever for my baby to come. I was so hungry and they told me I couldn't eat. I was in so much pain and wanted medicine, but mommy said no because she never used it with any of us. I cried and cried and cried some more, until she realized I couldn't take it anymore and my heart rate was dropping. After they gave me the medicine I was chilling. We played cards and laughed until the doctor checked me and said it was time. I pushed and pushed for a hour and I wasn't even pushing right, so I started getting frustrated. My mom noticed and told me how to push. After the baby came out I started loosing so much blood, and I remembered going in and out. I tried my hardest to keep my eyes opened just enough to see my mom holding her. After I saw my mom holding her and she said she was perfect I heard the doctor saying I was losing too much blood, then I blacked out.

When I woke up I saw my mother sleeping next to me on a chair, but I did not see my baby. So I woke my mother up and she went to try to go find her. When she came back into my room there was no baby in her hands, so I got really scared. She told me that they said I was too weak to get the baby. I said okay and sat there for ten minutes, and it felt like forever. So I tried to get up and my mom told me to stay, but I did not listen. I wanted my baby and I wanted her at that moment. When I stood up I immediately fainted to the floor, and the doctors carried me back to the bed. They told me I needed rest, so I fell asleep. When I woke up that's when I saw her, she was indeed perfect. She was 8lbs and 13 oz. of pure beauty. I named her D'ziyah. It means the same as the original desire, but with my little twist. Looking at her was like a dream and holding her reassured me that I was ready to do the mother thing. Her smell drove me crazy and her skin was so soft. I got my baby and I was happy.

God is powerful

∞∞∞

The next day mommy went home and checked on my sisters, but when she got back she looked like something was wrong. I was supposed to be released the next day. She told me that since I had the baby we couldn't stay in that shelter anymore, because our family size was too large for the whole shelter. She said we had to move to the Bronx. At first I didn't care as long as I had my family, but then I thought about Mrs. Woodward and my friends and got sad. She said we had to leave the same day I got out the hospital so I couldn't go back to my school. I didn't get too upset because I could always call Mrs. Woodward at the school and talk to her. I also could just bring the baby to see her. So I was ready.

The next day I got out the hospital and they took us back to the shelter to wait on our ride. While there we said goodbye to the other people in the shelter and the security guards. I let them see my baby and then we left. We arrived to our new shelter in the Bronx and it was big. It had a lot of rooms in it and that borough felt more like home to me. Everything was great until one day I got enough strength to take the baby back to Queens to see Mrs. Woodward, but when I called the school and asked to speak to her the administrator said she no longer worked there. I was confused so I asked to speak to the principal. The principal knew exactly who I was and explained to me that Mrs. Woodward had retired. I asked for her phone number, but she said she could not give it out to anyone. She asked me to give her my number and if she called she would tell her.

That phone call broke me inside, because she never got a chance to see my baby. I kept trying and trying and nothing. No calls or nothing. After one year I stop trying. At the time I did not understand any of it, but now I do. It's now been 15 years later and I still have not seen or heard from her. I do not know her first name either because at that time we were not allowed to call teachers by their first names. It's crazy that I remember this story like it was yesterday. I believe it's a reason for that. Sometimes God send people in your life just to help you or send out a message for him, and you may never see them again until needed. I have a vision that this book would end up in her hands and she will find and reach out to me. You see what's the odd of this happening, right? I say the same odds that brought us together in the first place. GOD!! I believe she will get to see D'ziyah and our bond will be like we never departed. Mrs. Woodward I thank God for you. I love you so much. You inspired me so much in my life and I can not wait until we meet again... The End......

Made in the USA
Columbia, SC
08 March 2020

88833437R00021